Follow His Instructions

A Message by

Evelyn Rainey

Copyright © 2024 Evelyn Rainey
Illustrations and Cover Design © 2024 Evelyn Rainey

All rights reserved. No part of this book may be reproduced, scanned, or distributed in any printed, audio or electronic form without permission. Such piracy of copyrighted materials is a violation of the author's rights and is punishable by law.

First presented at United Methodist Temple, Lakeland, FL August 18, 2024.

ISBN-13: 978-1-946469-88-5

ShelteringTree.Earth, LLC
PO Box 973, Eagle Lake, FL 33839
ShelteringTreeMedia.com

DEDICATION

For all heroes who have a flaw.

Pastoral Prayer

Dearest God, Utmost Divine, Holy Spirit, and Jesus the Christ,

We come today to praise your name and worship at your feet.

We ask you, Lord, to give us what we need: food, shelter, a place to belong, loved ones, and most importantly, a purpose in your kingdom. We ask for peace within our souls as we stand in a world of war. We ask for the ability to confer understanding in a world divided by deceit and betrayal. We ask for empathy in a world filled with apathy.

And we ask that You forgive us for the things we have done which were wrong. We ask you to forgive us for the things we did not do which we should have done. We ask you to forgive us for being cowards when you have shown us how to live courageously without fear.

In turn, let us forgive those who have abused us, those who have betrayed us, those who have hurt us intentionally or unintentionally.

We especially want to forgive those who just ignored us, as if we were not worthy of attention.

We ask for strength to face what is to come. To stand against the foe and fight for what is true and right. We know that the victory is yours – earned by your sacrifice and enjoyed by all who call on your name.

We ask especially that we learn how to follow your instructions. We have not earned your grace. We do not deserve your miracles. We are flawed. But if we follow your instructions, we will belong to you.

And now, together as the body and bride of Christ, we repeat the prayer you taught us:

Our Father, which art in heaven, hollowed be your name.
Thy kingdom come; thy will be done
On Earth as it is in heaven.
Give us this day our daily bread.
And forgive us our sins as we forgive those who sin against us.
And lead us not into temptation.
But deliver us from evil.

For thine is the kingdom, and the power, and the glory, forever.
   Amen.

Introduction

As a writer and a publisher, I know that each villain must have a virtue which redeems them, if only for a moment. And conversely, each hero must have a flaw with which the readers can identify.

In books, heroes are often remembered, not for the heroic things they do, but for what flaws they have. Jane Eyre was remembered, not for her strong moral character, but for her plain features. Cyrano de'Bergerac was remembered, not for his writing skills, but for his huge nose. The world sees flaws as definitions of the whole, rather than as interesting character development.

Luke 15:16 states:

But Jesus told them: You are always making yourselves look good, but God sees what is in your heart. The things that most people think are important are worthless as far as God is concerned.[1]

---

[1] All Scripture quoted in this message come from **Contemporary English Version (CEV)** 1995 by American Bible Society. www.bibles.com and www.cev.bible.

We were raised with these ideas:
Dress for Success
The Clothes Make the Man

We use clothes to define ourselves. But eventually, those clothes are going to become too small or too worn, or just plain dirty. And that becomes a problem.

When we have a problem, a pile of dirty clothes for example, we can't just ignore it. We can't just foist it off on someone else. We certainly can't expect help from the world. Stick it in the oven and you're going to have a worse mess than you had to begin with. The refrigerator is no better. We must sort out our laundry and place it in the only appliance that can clean it.

So, what should we do about our flaws?

Message

Follow His Instructions
Naaman & Elisha
Scripture: 2 Kings 5:1-16

1. Sort Things Out
2. Take Everything Out of Your Pockets
3. Follow the Directions

Sort Things Out

2 Kings 5:1-8

5 1 Naaman was the commander of the Syrian army. The LORD had helped him and his troops defeat their enemies, so the king of Syria respected Naaman very much. Naaman was a brave soldier, but he had leprosy.
2 One day while the Syrian troops were raiding Israel, they captured a girl, and she became a slave of Naaman's wife. 3 Sometime later the girl said, "If your husband Naaman would go to the prophet in Samaria, he would be cured of his leprosy."
4 When Naaman told the king what the girl had said, 5 the king replied, "Go ahead! I will give you a letter to take to the king of Israel."
Naaman left and took along 30,000 pieces of silver, 6,000 pieces of gold, and 10 new outfits. 6 He also carried the letter to the king of Israel. It said, "I am sending my General Naaman to you. Would you cure him of his leprosy?"
7 When the king of Israel read the letter, he tore his clothes in fear and shouted, "That Syrian king believes I can cure this man of leprosy! Does he think I'm God with power over life and death? He must be trying to pick a fight with me."

⁸As soon as Elisha the prophet heard what had happened, he sent the Israelite king this message: "Why are you so afraid? Send the man to me, so that he will know there is a prophet in Israel."

This is the Word of God, for the People of God; thanks be to God.

Sort Things Out

slave girl from Israel ➡ Naaman's wife ➡ king of Syria ⬇ king of Israel ⬅ prophet in Israel

The first part of this passage shows how the world worked, and still works today. There was a man, a great man, talented, an asset to his boss, famous in some circles even, but he had a problem. And he didn't know what to do about it. At first, he ignored it. But it didn't go away.

Then he heard about a way to cure it. Instead of following the directions the young slave girl gave him – he turned to his king and asked him what to do.

Naaman ignored the answer that God had provided.

The king, thinking in worldly terms, contacted the king of Israel, asking for his help. He misinterpreted the instructions. He didn't know who the prophet of Israel was. He applied knowledge instead of wisdom to the problem.

The king of Israel, sorting things out in worldly terms, envisioned this request as a plot to entrap and belittle him, and got mad. He was useless in the process of cleaning up this mess.

But the man **who knew God**, knew God's ways, and listened to the world but applied wisdom to the world's knowledge, requested that Naaman be sent to him.

And Naaman came. He finally got his problem sorted out in the right place. It wouldn't be the world that would solve his problem, **it would be God.**

Take Everything Out of Your Pockets

Naaman took with him *"ten talents of silver, six thousand shekels of gold and ten sets of clothing. And his horses and chariots. And servants"* to go see Elisha. You know what else he took with him?

His leprosy.

```
= enough to feed a family for 1789
years, or 1789 families for one year
```

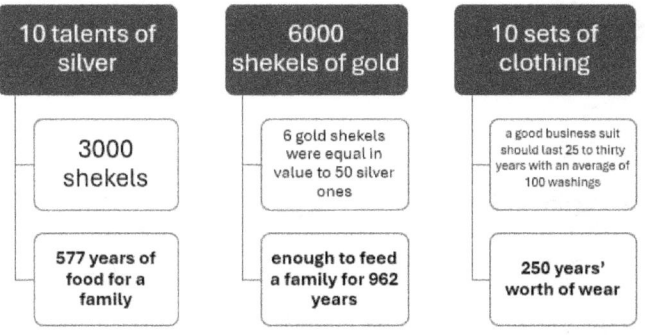

Let's take a look at what Naaman brought with him as a bribe

Ten talents of silver

1 talent silver = 30 kilo = 3000 shekels; "A single silver shekel was enough to support a small

family for about one week."[2] therefore, **the silver Naaman brought was worth 577 years of food for a family.**

Six thousand shekels of gold

Just "six gold shekels were equal in value to 50 silver ones."[3]

So, 6000 shekels of gold = 50,000 shekels of silver. **Therefore, Naaman brought enough gold to feed a family for 962 years.**

Ten sets of clothing

According to the writer of the blog Splurge Frugal, a good business suit should last 25 to thirty years with an average of 100 washings.[4] Therefore,

---

[2] Talent of Silver. https://www.answers.com/Q/How_much_is_a_talent_of_silver_worth_in_dollars

[3] https://www.learnreligions.com/shekel-worth-its-weight-in-gold-3977062

[4] https://splurgefrugal.com/how-long-should-a-suit-last-does-it-matter/ and https://www.styleforum.net/threads/how-long-do-you-expect-a-suit-to-last.206585/

Naaman's ten sets of clothes represents almost **250 years' worth of wear.**

TOTAL SUM OF BRIBE in Years: 577+962+250 = enough to support a family for 1789 years. Or 1789 families for one year.

But remember, that's not all Naaman brought with him; he brought his flaw. Let's take a look at Leprosy.[5]

If left untreated, the signs of advanced leprosy can include:

- Paralysis and crippling of hands and feet
- Shortening of toes and fingers due to reabsorption
- Chronic non-healing ulcers on the bottoms of the feet
- Blindness
- Loss of eyebrows
- Nose disfigurement

Other complications that may sometimes occur are:

---

[5] https://www.cdc.gov/leprosy/symptoms/index.html

- Painful or tender nerves
- Redness and pain around the affected area
- Burning sensation in the skin

Being Healed from Leprosy = Priceless

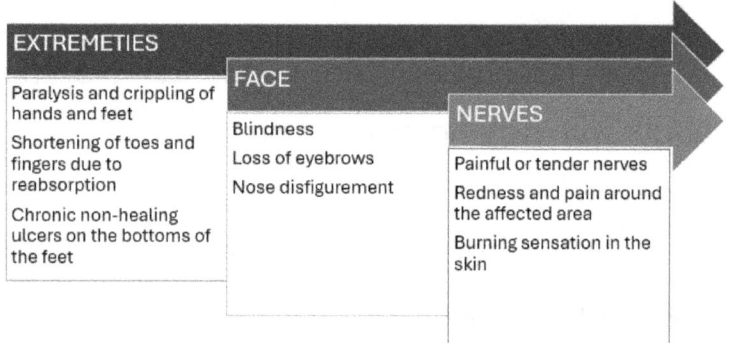

For a warrior, the paralysis and crippling of hands and feet, and blindness would leave him unable to fight. Loss of career, prestige, limbs, life. **Priceless**.

When you wash your laundry, especially if you have children, it is wise to check the pockets before tossing them in the machine. Pockets are what we use to carry things we think are valuable — stones and feathers gathered along a walk, dollar bills and receipts wadded up and stuffed inside after a purchase, safety pins and hair barrettes, business cards and grocery lists.

If we don't clean out our pockets of what we think is important before we wash our clothes, we lose them, or they can ruin the machine.

Naaman brought enough stuff with him to support 1789 families for a year. But he also brought his flaw with him. Only one thing was the most important – the leprosy he needed to have cured.

Naaman needed to empty everything out of his pockets before he washed.

Follow the Directions

We know how to get our clothes clean: put them in the washing machine.

I like to crochet with acrylic yarns. They are hypoallergenic, color fast, and wash and dry in almost any temperature without shrinkage. I can't say the same thing for wool or silk. I love cotton, but it has to be washed in cold water and dried in medium to low heat.

Who has not made the mistake of mixing a red shirt in with white clothes and coming out with pink? It happens to the best of us.

And who has not tried to use dishwashing soap in place of laundry detergent? In a moment of realization that you no longer have enough detergent, you grab for the closest thing. But you only do that one time, because, as you know, you'll spend the next six hours mopping up suds.

Know How to Read the Directions

I bet if you felt around the back of the collar or side of your shirt, you'll find a tag that solves most of your laundry problems – the washing instructions. They are usually in international symbols.

X over the triangle with the handle means don't iron.

The circle inside the square means it can be put in the dryer.

Dry clean only means what it says.

I'm not sure what the triangle with perpendicular lines means. Do you?[6]

---

[6] Thank you, Minter Goodson, for finding out this *means do not use bleach*.

Follow the directions. Your dirty clothes will come clean. Problem solved.

Scripture: 2 Kings 5:10-14

¹⁰ Elisha sent a messenger to say to him, "Go, wash yourself seven times in the Jordan, and your flesh will be restored and you will be cleansed."

¹¹ But Naaman went away angry and said, "I thought that he would surely come out to me and stand and call on the name of the Lord his God, wave his hand over the spot and cure me of my leprosy. ¹² Are not Abana and Pharpar, the rivers of Damascus, better than all the waters of Israel? Couldn't I wash in them and be cleansed?" So he turned and went off in a rage.

¹³ Naaman's servants went to him and said, "My father, if the prophet had told you to do some great thing, would you not have done it? How much more, then, when he tells you, **'Wash and be cleansed'!"** *¹⁴ So he went down and dipped himself in the Jordan seven times, as the man of God had told him, and* *his flesh was restored and became clean like that of a young boy.*

Naaman was given a set of instructions: **wash in the Jordan River seven times.** Not too difficult to understand. But he got upset. He got insulted. Here he was with this life altering problem and enough bribery to impress anyone; **he expected a little razzle dazzle.**

Here he was, a Great General of a Great Nation; **a little flash would be nice.**

Naaman was a rich man and armies trembled before him; was it too much to ask that he got healed in the midst of cheering crowds with an angel chorus?

Elisha didn't even come out to look him in the face!

Naaman might have believed, like some of us may believe: miracles should be larger than life!

Give me some pizzazz! Some drama and drum rolls, please!

Here Naaman was, prepared to hand over a fortune, and Elisha refused to accept it!

Some people believe tithing and sacrifice should be required before you can be washed clean.

And maybe conversely, if we sacrifice and tithe, **shouldn't God consider us already washed clean**?

No, God doesn't owe us anything. We owe God obedience. We need to follow His directions. And then yes, we can be washed clean.

You mean all I have to do is – **follow the instructions?**

Just wash. Just get clean. Clean yourself up the way God tells you to do. Follow His directions.

Well, you may ask what God's instructions are.

And I'll tell you:

"Hear o Israel, the Lord your God, the Lord is one, and you shall love the Lord your God with all your heart, with all your mind, with all your

soul, with all your strength, and love your neighbor as much as you love yourself."[7]

"Seek first the kingdom of God"[8] – that's another way to follow God's instructions.

We used to sing this set of instructions every Sunday. Please join with me if you will:

Praise God from whom all blessings flow.
Praise Him all creatures here below.
Praise Him above ye heavenly host.
Praise Father, Son, and Holy Ghost.[9]

Jesus instructed us to: Give food to the hungry. Give water to the thirsty. Welcome the stranger. Clothe the needy. Take care of the sick. Go out of your way to meet with those who are in prison. [10]

---

[7] Mark 12:28-30
[8] Matthew 6:33
[9] **Praise God, from whom all blessings flow,** Thomas Ken (1674) Tune: OLD HUNDREDTH, hymnary.org/text/praise_god_from_whom_all_blessings_ken
[10] Matthew 25: 35-36

And never forget this set of instructions:

*Truly, truly, I say to you, whoever **hears my word** and **believes Him who sent me** has eternal life. He does not come into judgment but has passed from death to life.*[11]

---

[11] John 5:24

Conclusion

In order to follow His instructions, you must:

1. **Sort Things Out** – figure out who to listen to. Are they advising you from the world's point of view or from God's?
2. **Take Everything Out of Your Pockets** – and determine which things are nice and which things are priceless
3. **Follow the Directions** – don't complain about it; don't be insulted by its simplicity, don't expect a chorus of angels to descend from above. Just do it.

Some of us are villains who have a few redeeming virtues, but most of us are heroes who have a flaw that needs to be healed.

Follow His Instructions, and your flaws will be washed clean.

Benediction

As you leave this sanctuary, this safe place of prayer, praise, and worship, and go into the world to begin your life anew, remember that:

Christ is with you,

Christ goes before you,

Christ supports behind you,

Christ is on your right,

Christ is on your left,

Christ will flow through you in all that you do.

Go in peace.

Hymns, Scriptures and Holy Writings

Hymn of Praise
Wash, O God, Our Sons and Daughters, Words: Ruth Duck, 1987, Music: Attr. To BF White 1844, harm. By Ronald A. Nelson, 1978, *United Methodist Hymnal #605*, (The United Methodist Publishing House, Nashville) 1989.

Hymn of Preparation
If Thou but Suffer God to Guide Thee, United Methodist Hymnal #142, WORDS & MUSIC: Georg Neumark, 1657, (The United Methodist Publishing House, Nashville) 1989.

Closing Hymn
I'm Gonna Sing When the Spirit Says Sing, United Methodist Hymnal #333, WORDS & MUSIC: Afro-American spiritual, adapted by William Farley Smith, 1986 (The United Methodist Publishing House, Nashville) 1989.

2 Kings 5:1-14

5 Naaman was the commander of the Syrian army. The LORD *had helped him and his troops defeat their enemies, so the king of Syria respected Naaman very much. Naaman was a brave soldier, but he had leprosy.*

² One day while the Syrian troops were raiding Israel, they captured a girl, and she became a servant of Naaman's wife. ³ Some time later the girl said, "If your husband Naaman would go to the prophet in Samaria, he would be cured of his leprosy."

⁴ When Naaman told the king what the girl had said, ⁵ the king replied, "Go ahead! I will give you a letter to take to the king of Israel."

Naaman left and took along 30,000 pieces of silver, 6,000 pieces of gold, and 10 new outfits. ⁶ He also carried the letter to the king of Israel. It said, "I am sending my servant Naaman to you. Would you cure him of his leprosy?"

⁷ When the king of Israel read the letter, he tore his clothes in fear and shouted, "That Syrian king believes I can cure this man of leprosy! Does he think I'm God with power over life and death? He must be trying to pick a fight with me."

⁸ As soon as Elisha the prophet heard what had happened, he sent the Israelite king this message: "Why are you so afraid? Send the man to me, so that he will know there is a prophet in Israel."

⁹ Naaman left with his horses and chariots and stopped at the door of Elisha's house. ¹⁰ Elisha sent someone outside to say to him, "Go wash seven times in the Jordan River. Then you'll be completely cured."

¹¹ But Naaman stormed off, grumbling, "Why couldn't he come out and talk to me? I thought for sure he would stand in front of me and pray to the LORD *his God, then wave his hand over my skin and cure me.* ¹² *What about the Abana River or the Pharpar River? Those rivers in Damascus are just as good as any river in Israel. I could have washed in them and been cured."*

¹³ *His servants went over to him and said, "Sir, if the prophet had told you to do something difficult, you would have done it. So why don't you do what he said? Go wash and be cured."*

¹⁴ *Naaman walked down to the Jordan; he waded out into the water and stooped down in it seven times, just as Elisha had told him. At once, he was cured, and his skin became as smooth as a child's.*

Luke 15:16

But Jesus told them: You are always making yourselves look good, but God sees what is in your heart. The things that most people think are important are worthless as far as God is concerned.

ABOUT THE AUTHOR

Evelyn Rainey has always loved to tell stories and help others understand. As such, she is a published author & educator. But she is also a papaya gardener, cat wrangler, and crochet artist. She manages **ShelteringTree.Earth, LLC Publishing** and facilitates the **Prayer Shawl Ministry** and the **Senior Adults Program** at the **United Methodist Temple** in Lakeland, Florida, as well as serving on the **SPRC**. She is in the process of becoming a Licensed Local Pastor through the United Methodist Church.

After 38 years in education, Evelyn retired after having earned BS degrees and Certificates of Endorsement in Early Childhood Education, Elementary Education, Gifted Education, Integrated Middle School Curriculum, English for Speakers of Other Languages, and Journalism. She has taught all grade levels from Kindergarten through Adult and at many different facilities, including jails and teen pregnancy centers. From

2019-2024, she was her mother's full-time caregiver.

Evelyn has over a dozen books published including science fiction, fantasy, historical fiction, new age urban fantasy, metaphysical and visionary, pastoral handbooks, and children's books. She currently has a list of a dozen new projects she plans to have published over the next few years. She has facilitated writer groups (and continues to do so with on-line meetings and would love you to join them (see ShelteringTreeMedia.com/events). She has been guest speaker and guest author at writer conferences and conventions throughout the southeast US.

Her love of teaching has expanded into videos for book trailers, crochet lessons, meditation series, Bible studies, as well as interviews and writing lessons. (See her YouTube channel **evelynrainey4780**.)

Evelyn is able to conduct interviews and conferences via phone and video communication (zoom, duo, etc.) She is also able to travel to conventions and special book events. She welcomes questions and comments from her readers but prefers to be contacted initially through https://evelynrainey.com/contact.

DISCUSSION GUIDE FOR BOOK CLUBS, JOURNALING, OR PERSONAL CONTEMPLATION

Write or discuss your answers.

1. Are you famous for something? What is your greatest achievement?

2. What is your greatest flaw?

3. Who do you turn to for advice? Why?

4. Have you ever asked God for advice? Did you follow His advice or not? What was the result?

_____

_____

_____

_____

_____

_____

_____

_____

5. Describe the slave girl's purpose in this story. How would Naaman's life have changed if she had not become enslaved?

6. What would you be willing to pay for complete health for yourself? For someone else?

_____

_____

_____

_____

_____

_____

_____

_____

_____

7. In your opinion, what is the worst disease or physical disability there is? Why?

8. What are some of the things you need to sort out in your life before you can follow God's instructions?

_____

_____

_____

_____

_____

_____

_____

_____

_____

9. Explain the directions Elisha gave to Naaman. Why seven? Why the Jordan River? What other significance did these instructions hold? Was this baptism?

10. Why didn't Elisha come out to meet with Naaman? Give three possible reasons.

11. In what ways does your faith reflect on your participation in your church or synagogue (attending each service, tithing, volunteering, dress codes, proper behavior in the sanctuary, etc.)?

12. Have you ever witnessed or received a miracle? Describe and explain it.

13. Do you think some people deserve miracles? If so, do you also believe that some people do not deserve miracles? Explain your opinion.

_____

_____

_____

_____

_____

_____

_____

_____

_____

14. Do you need a miracle? What is it? What do you think is preventing that miracle from being manifested?

_____

_____

_____

_____

_____

_____

_____

_____

_____

15. Most people who win the lottery are penniless within the next five years.[12] What do you think happens to people who receive miracles? Can you name some or give examples?

---

[12] Nathan Gibson. 12 Reasons Why Most Lottery Winners Recklessly Blow Through All Their Cash.
https://www.ranker.com/list/why-most-lottery-winners-blow-through-their-money/nathan-gibson

16. How do you think God's healing of Naaman's leprosy changed Naaman's life?

17. How do you think God's healing of Naaman's leprosy changed the king of Israel's life?

18. How do you think God's healing of Naaman's leprosy changed the king of Syria's life?

19. How do you think God's healing of Naaman's leprosy changed the slave girl's life?

20. How do you think God's healing of Naaman's leprosy changed your life?

_____

_____

_____

_____

_____

_____

_____

_____

_____

We publish books, videos, audios, & podcasts to help you feed His sheep.

Visit

ShelteringTreeMedia.com

for more information.

www.ingramcontent.com/pod-product-compliance
Lightning Source LLC
Chambersburg PA
CBHW072037060426
42449CB00010BA/2312